Writing as

The term "writing" is commonly used to describe both the act of articulating thoughts on paper (or its electronic equivalent) and the product of that process of articulation. This can create confusion in advice about writing. Are we talking about the product or the process? Which one should we be talking about?

Scientists have stopped debating whether light is a particle or a wave and accepted that it is both at the same time, even though you can only deal with it as a particle or a wave at any particular time. I suggest we do the same in our discussion of writing.

**Writing is a process through which you
create knowledge.
AND
Writing is a product that
communicates knowledge.**

To understand how to improve both process and product, we need to separate them heuristically. The process of communicating your work with others (which we call publication) goes on at the same time as the process of developing your ideas and arguments so that they are fit to be communicated with others. Neither the process nor the product is more important. Sometimes you focus on the process. Other times you focus on the product/publication. The shift in focus becomes a kind of dance.

Furthermore, because writing is so tied up with your identity, many of your struggles with writing are emotional. You have an emotional attachment to being competent, to being right, to being a good writer, to being part of a discipline/field/etc. You may also have an emotional connection to the topic you write about.

The emotional vulnerability of writing affects your writing process. Procrastination and distraction are often rooted in the desire to avoid writing that is emotionally difficult in some way. Perfectionism is often an attempt to protect yourself from painful criticism. It isn't (just) the writing that is difficult but all the emotional processing that goes along with it that holds you back.

One of the members of the Academic Writing Studio reminded me that you don't always need to know how to solve a problem to move forward. Being able to state the problem clearly often shifts things enough to allow movement. It doesn't help to push your emotions away and pretend that the issue you face is merely a technical one that any good writer could overcome easily.

Is there an emotional element to your current stuck?

Problems with motivation and concentration often have emotional roots.

Why did you start this project?

Were you ever excited about it? What was exciting about it?

If it was never exciting, is this a project that feels less risky (in some way) than the writing you really get excited about? Is it so safe that even you aren't that interested in it? Do you have to finish it?

Can you identify one thing about this project that you are interested in enough to keep you going?

Does this project feel risky somehow? List the risks. Even the exaggerated ones the gremlins see. Go through the list asking: Is this true? Is it likely? Would I be able to handle it if it did happen?

Does this project feed your need for an intellectual home? Does the direction your writing seems to be taking you threaten your belonging in that particular intellectual space?

Is this a collaborative project? Do you value the relationship with the collaborators more than the project itself? Or is the relationship with your collaborators holding you back from taking your writing in a particular direction?

Is there another question you wish I'd asked? Ask yourself and answer it. Also feel free to reword any of those questions. The idea is to be clear on what the emotional difficulty is so you can decide what to do about it.

Some strategies:

Write your way through the difficulty. It is not a waste of time to write things that you will not share (even with your collaborators). You might need to write it to figure out the part you do feel safe sharing.

You don't have to finish everything you start. You don't have to publish everything you write. Your writing project is bigger than the specific publications that will come out of it.

It's okay to pick the safer product. It's also okay to take risks. Trust your judgement. I know academics who have taken over 20 years to publish something that felt too risky at the time.

JO VAN EVERY

You don't have to be monogamous. If one of your writing projects is a duty project, also work on a project that you are really excited about. Alternate between them. You can do the same to mitigate the risks of a more risky project; work on something safer at the same time.

Consider counselling or therapy to deal with perfectionism and/or fear of criticism, especially if it makes it impossible for you to share things, even with trusted friends and colleagues.

Beginnings

Just as light isn't only a wave but sometimes needs to be treated as a wave, there are times when it is absolutely right to treat writing as a process whose value is determined by the quality of your intellectual and creative experience of doing it. Beginning is one of those times.

The first stage of the writing process involves getting the ideas onto paper (or its electronic equivalent) in a form where you can develop them. Writing isn't some purely technical process of getting already coherent ideas out of your head and into the world. It is a cognitive process in which you figure out what you might have to say, and to whom. Trying to avoid writing incoherent thoughts and/or avoiding writing until you know what the product is going to be are major contributors to writer's block. You are not abandoning your commitment to academic standards or to publishing by doing this. You are allowing yourself to use writing to think. You are engaging in an intellectual and creative process.

Gremlins have some kind of irrational fear of shitty first drafts. They don't want you to have to revise. Ever. Except maybe some spelling mistakes and typos.

But that's not how writing works. Writing is rewriting. Rewriting is writing. Shitty first drafts are an essential part of the process.

Curiosity about how your thoughts will develop is enough to start writing. You don't have to know what kind of writing product (book, article, blog post, etc) this will eventually become.

The spark that gets you started may be a conversation you are having in your head prompted by an article or book you have read, something said on social media or in the pub or the corridor, something you saw on the news, or something in a conference presentation. Your curiosity might be piqued by the juxtaposition of two different things you've read or heard, by something you've noticed in your data, or by wondering what happens if you take this theory and use it to think about sources you are familiar with. All of these are good starting points, even if some or all of them are not great ending points. I was inspired to write this *Short Guide* when I found myself talking to a book review Rohan Maitzen wrote in *Open Letters Monthly*. She had been similarly inspired: "the further I read in Gilbert's book, the more I wanted to argue with it, to respond to it, to review it."

There may be many beginnings. There is the very seed of a beginning when you are considering a brand new topic or field. But there are also other beginnings: that arise during the process. The point when you wonder what would happen if you went in this direction. (Rather than that one. Or just because a new direction has presented itself.) The point where the writing is generating more questions than answers and you need to figure out what belongs in the current project and what might become a new project. The point where you think maybe this is a journal article, you imagine a particular reader, and you are curious about what it means to write for this particular journal/reader. The point where you wonder if the problem with whatever-you-are-writing is that it is actually two articles rather than the one article you thought it was. Or when you wonder whether there is a book in here after all. Or maybe what you thought was a book, turns out not to really be a book.

Just because the beginning and the ending are not always clear doesn't mean you don't have somewhere to start.

Not sure what to write about?

Indulge your curiosity about your topic. Make a list. Right now. Just write. Don't overthink.

What are you curious about?

What could you be writing?

Look at your list:

Does anything on this list surprise you?

Does anything on this list excite you?

Does anything on this list terrify you?

Or try these:

Write out your important questions.

Write out your thoughts even though they are not fully formed.

Write reflective notes on something you've read.

Write your take(s) on the questions that sparked your desire to write.

Not sure *how* to get started?

You may even indulge your curiosity about the process itself.

What happens if you draw? Diagrams, pictures, ...

What happens if you dictate your ideas while you are walking?

Does it matter where you start? Or if you jump around arbitrarily?

If your gremlins think that once you start a Scrivener project or create a Word document you have a project that needs a clear outcome and deadlines and Must Be Finished, there are a few strategies for working around them:

Write in a paper notebook with a pen. Call it an "ideas" book.

Write on scrap paper with crayons. Something that tells your gremlins you are just playing.

Give yourself time to do this playful, curious writing regularly. This is where new projects and brilliant insights come from. Seeds don't look like the plant they eventually grow into.

Moving Your Project Forward

Writing is a complex process. It involves articulating ideas and thoughts into words, refining those words into a (usually linear) narrative, and then a whole lot of fiddly tasks that make that writing publishable in a particular form (references, headings, subheadings, bibliography, etc). You can give those types of writing different names like generative writing, revision, editing, proofreading, etc. Or, you can just accept that writing involves a lot of different kinds of work and if it moves your project forward, this task counts.

The process isn't really linear. You may go back and forth between putting more ideas on paper in very rough form and refining the ones you've got on paper into something more coherent. Software like Scrivener or Evernote that allows you to write in small chunks and then rearrange, split, and merge bits of writing as you refine your arguments can really help at this stage. Don't allow your gremlins to tell you that you should be able to do this in your head and only commit your ideas to paper when they are clear. Use writing to think.

You will also go back and forth between various forms of writing and other activities that contribute to the process of articulating and refining your ideas and arguments: Reading. Analysing data. Mulling things over. Or just leaving your project alone for a while so you can get some perspective. It can be hard to tell whether your project really needs something that doesn't look like writing to move forward or whether you are resisting writing by doing something else.

Write early. Write often. Write what you know now. Make notes you know are incomplete or possibly erroneous. Makes notes to check things. But write. Lots of words. Crappy words you can rewrite later.

You will still be treating writing purely as an intellectual and creative process for a while. Indulge your curiosity. Allow yourself to go off on interesting tangents for at least long enough to see how interesting they might be. You don't know what this writing is going to be yet (nor do you need to). You are using writing to help you articulate your arguments more clearly.

YOU need to drive the narrative. The whole point of writing this is to express your opinion. It will be your educated opinion, based on the research you've done and the literature in your field. But it will be yours. If reading, analysing more data, or walking away for a bit helps you make a stronger argument, do that. If those activities are a way of calming your fear that what you have to say isn't worth saying, write.

To appease the gremlin who thinks you never finish anything, schedule a time to come back to the writing (on this project). Pay attention to any surges of energy compelling you to return to it. That might be a Eureka! moment, or just insistent curiosity about the project.

Not sure what to do next?

I strongly encourage you to write the thing you most want to write. Not the safest thing. Not the thing you think you should write. The part that you are most excited about and need to get out of your head. Trust the process.

If you'd like a more structured way to make this decision, try this. When you sit down to write set a timer for 1 minute and ask yourself,

> "What does this writing project need to move forward?"

Write down everything that comes to mind, no matter how ridiculous. Your list will probably be a list of gremlin admonishments, your own deep desires, and actual tasks. Select the task on that list that you most want to do (for whatever reason; that isn't always the most fun thing). Even if there is a gremlin saying that this "isn't really writing", it will move your writing project closer to finished so it counts. Start there.

Do you need to read or are you reading to procrastinate?

Fear tries to prevent you from writing anything at all before you've done more reading. If that's what's happening, go back to the section on Beginnings, and write out some answers to the prompts there.

If you've started and are stuck, reading might well be the thing your project needs to move forward.

Option 1: Read to fix one of those spots that you aren't sure about. Read enough to fix it. Then write the new version. Then find another spot that needs fixing. Read enough to fix it. Write the new version. Rinse. Repeat.

Corollary to Option 1: If you are in flow but know you need to read more, make a note to yourself in your text about what you need to read and why. Keep writing. Go back another day and address the note.

Option 2: Read. Write reflective notes on what you are reading. In particular reflect on how this affects the argument you have been making.

Option 2 can also be used even if you think your desire to read comes out of fear. It's okay to be afraid. If reading is something you can do today, read. Write about what you are reading. Try to go beyond summary to curious reflection.

Are you fidgeting or restless?

If you are having difficulty concentrating when you sit down to write, and that lack of focus manifests itself as fidgeting or restlessness, that is a sign that you need to do something physical. Your brain works better when you are moving. You can just get up and do physical activity for a short (timed?) period and go back to writing. However, you can also mull over your project while taking a long walk, doing physical labour (raking leaves, gardening, cleaning the house) or other activity that keeps you busy but doesn't use the same brain space as your writing project. You probably want to keep some means of recording insights nearby. You can even experiment with dictation software so that you can record your insights orally and easily incorporate them into your draft later.

Does this project need a time out?

If you have lost perspective and can't figure out what to do next, your project might need to be left alone for a while. If it's in a state where someone else might provide feedback, then give it to someone else to look at and go on to something else. If you aren't ready to show it to anyone, just put it aside for a while. Work on a different project.

Schedule a time to come back to it. In your first session after a break from a project your goal is to refamiliarize yourself with the draft, make notes on what it needs, and maybe make some big decisions. Although it will be a bit difficult to get back into it, you will also be seeing it with a different perspective and that will help it move forward.

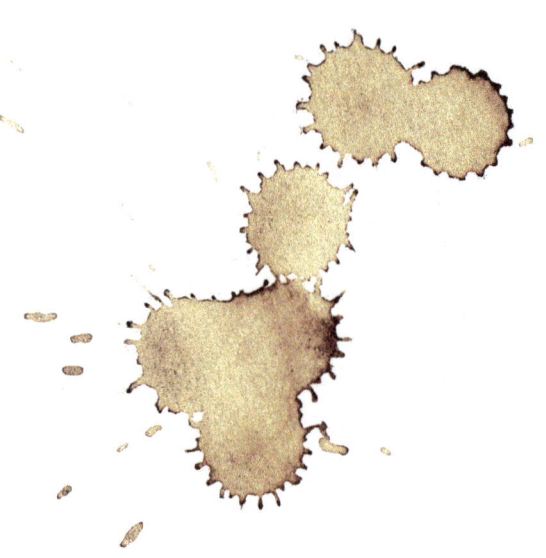

From Process to Product: Who Are You Writing For?

Once you have words on a page, and you've developed them a bit so that they are somewhat coherent words, the balance between process and product will shift. As your argument becomes clearer, the product takes on a more concrete form.

> Think of publishing in the broadest sense of the word. A transfer from brain to brain, via some sort of tool. (Margaret Atwood)

The validation narrative has become the narrative frame for discussing academic publishing — Will this count? How will this count? Am I wasting my time writing this if it won't count? — and yet, a scholarly journal is but one tool you can use to transfer knowledge from your brain to the brains of other scholars. You may also communicate to a variety of audiences, not just scholars. You will likely use a variety of tools, both written and oral, to communicate your knowledge. Some of those tools are more formal than others and their status in various validation processes varies considerably.

You may notice that there is more than one direction this piece of writing could take. Your writing will result in more than one product. Those writing products may be sequential — a conference paper that will later become a journal article — or complementary — several journal articles focused on different arguments, or a journal article for scholarly readers and a different kind of piece for a specific non-academic audience.

This is another sort of beginning. Until this point your primary focus has been on the intellectual satisfaction you gain from the process. You now need to consider your reader. No matter how intellectually satisfying the process is, you started writing this because there were things you wanted to say. You write to participate in a conversation, albeit a rather formal, asynchronous conversation that may include dead people. My own thinking about publication as communication was heavily influenced by this passage by Dorothy E Smith:

> In the early seventies I had written a paper entitled "Women's Perspective as a Radical Critique of Sociology," which I presented at a conference at the University of Oregon. Thereafter it circulated in an extraordinary manner in draft. I got letters from all over, including one, to my astonishment, from Hungary. I could not understand how a paper that had never been published could circulate so widely. It made me aware for the first time that when I wrote a paper for an academic context of presentation or publication I might actually be speaking to people. It made me aware of the possibility of using academic sites of discourse and of writing for academic occasions

in ways quite different from my earlier understanding of their uses. Previously I think I had always seen producing papers as a performance for invisible judges. Writing papers for publication made me nervous. Sometimes I used to take a slug of brandy to get me going. My experience with how that paper traveled changed my view altogether. I saw that a paper could be a way of reaching other women, of talking to them. The academic linkages could be used as a medium of communication among women. I saw that I did not have to write a finally complete and perfected piece of work, but that I could write as I went along to tell other women, "this is the work I've been doing; this is where I've got to; this is how it looks right now; how does it look to you?" I understood that a discourse could be organized differently than one organized around an establishment that judged and controlled and held its practitioners to conform to its notions of how sociology should be practiced. I saw that the academic media could be used as a medium to reach other women and to hear from them.

Set aside your performance anxiety about "producing papers as a performance for invisible judges" and allow yourself to be curious about publishing as communication for a little while.

In order to decide what writing products might coalesce from your writing process, you need to identify who you want to engage in conversation — the potential reader of your writing product — and what you have to contribute to a particular conversation. You will also consider the various tools available to you to communicate your increasingly well articulated arguments to that reader. You may redefine what you think of as your writing project at this point, creating one with a narrower focus on producing a specific product that will be shared (published) with specific others in some way.

Fear might try to rein in your curiosity as you do this: Fear that no one will care about your work. Fear that you don't know how to reach these particular readers. Fear that these readers won't count in the validation process.

If this happens, stop. Take a few deep breaths. Answering these questions does not commit you to actually publishing a writing product for any of the readers you identify. You are just being curious about who might benefit from the ideas you are writing about right now.

Your gremlins may also get in on the act here, perhaps suggesting people they think you should be writing for. You may decide to write down their suggestions along with your own. If you do, you may want to note which suggestions came from the gremlins.

Who might read what you are writing?

Don't think too hard about this. Write down everyone that comes to mind. Write quickly, without stopping, until you run out of ideas: very specific individuals (e.g. the author of another article), types of individual (e.g. scholars in a specific field, a particular type of practitioner, general readers of particular kinds of books), everyone.

Who would benefit from your work?

Whose work or life would be better for knowing what you've been working on?

Whose work has influenced the writing you have been doing?

Who are you already (implicitly) talking to as you write? (It's okay if they are dead. Or famous. Or, equally, if they are not scholars, or not fashionable.)

To whom would you like to say "this is the work I've been doing; this is where I've got to; this is how it looks right now; how does it look to you?"

Look at your initial responses and develop them further to get a better idea of your potential readers. Break down big categories into smaller ones. Expand individuals to consider them as a type.

Set your list aside and come back to it another day to make a decision about where to start. Sleep is actually magical. Your brain does important work while you are sleeping so if you put this list aside for now and come back to it tomorrow or another day soon, you will see it differently than if you plow on right now. Go do something else. Work on another project, or even on something different from writing. Sleep. The next time you open this project, you can make some decisions.

Determining Which Writing Products to Prioritize

In the previous section you created a preliminary list of who you want to be communicating with. Your list might be quite short. There is no right or wrong way for this list to look. The thing you are working on might only be of interest to one kind of potential reader, or it might be relevant to a few different kinds of potential reader. The types of potential reader on your list might be mostly scholarly, or mostly some particular kind of non-scholarly reader. You are just being curious about whose knowledge you want to advance with this particular piece of writing, and perhaps whether this thing you are working on is one writing product or several.

You don't need to write for all of these possible readers. You get to choose. You do not have to decide all the possible products of this writing project at the outset. And you may find that initial products generate interest that brings you back to the project and changes your publication priorities. Because writing is part of an ongoing conversation, you may want to communicate with some readers first to help you refine your writing further, and then communicate with others. Knowing what you'd like to do allows you to make better decisions.

It is important to note that even when you have identified a relatively bounded set of questions, evidence, and arguments, you will probably publish multiple products. The tools you have available include blog posts, conference papers, seminar papers, working papers, journal articles, and books. Some publishing tools are more suited to some purposes than others. And some readers prefer different types of publishing tool. You get to prioritize which readers you will write for. Your stage of career and your own career goals will influence your priorities.

You may discover that while you think a particular argument will be important for a particular reader, you are not confident that you are ready to communicate with them yet. You may need to produce an interim product, some kind of work in progress publishing or presentation that enables you to get feedback before publishing something more substantial. Publishing will both communicate your ideas and arguments and contribute to your process of developing those arguments. Or, it could be that certain audiences will be more likely to listen to what you have to say if they know that your knowledge claims have been validated by your peers.

You also want to consider how the reader is going to find out that your work exists. Do not assume you know how they do that, even if your prospective reader is a scholar in your field. I once ran a workshop in which

I asked a group of scholars how things got on their "to read" list and the answers were quite diverse. Many people in the room were somewhat surprised by what they heard from their colleagues.

Here are some issues to take into account when communicating with other scholars. The fact that journals are indexed and abstracted in databases means that they are more likely to be found in searches than, say, chapters in edited books. Conference papers, blog posts, and other less formal ways of disseminating work in progress also create an interest in your work that may lead readers to your published work. Some scholars have a limited set of journals that they routinely look at to see what's coming out. Many scholars follow specific authors seeking out other work (past and future) by those whose work they find interesting.

For non-academic audiences, be careful not to make assumptions about the priority of (certain types of) writing based on your own organizational culture. Reading and writing are central to your job and you have trouble finding time to do them. Other readers may appreciate longer written pieces, but find it easier to find time to engage with shorter pieces of writing, video, or audio. If your goal is to influence practice, it may be more effective to run workshops or produce training materials, both of which may require other products to build an interest in those more detailed forms. Don't guess. Research what will be most effective.

What kind of product would best communicate with this reader?

You'll need the list of potential readers you created using the questions at the end of the previous section.

When you look at your list, is there a particular potential reader that stands out?

Start with this reader.

What difference do you want this particular piece of writing to make to that reader?

Why do you think this reader would be interested in your work?

How would knowing about your work benefit this reader?

What do you know about how this reader finds out about new knowledge / research?

What tools could you use to communicate with this particular reader? (List everything that comes to mind. You can pick one later.)

Does this reader care whether your writing has been validated by peers? What might that mean?

Is there a way to get feedback from this type of reader prior to formal publication?

If this is a reader you are less familiar with, how could you learn more about them and how they learn?

You don't need to determine all the possible products before you decide which product to take forward to the next stage of the process. I strongly encourage you to start with the reader who stood out for you intuitively. This is who you really WANT to be writing for. Once you have created that first product and sent it on to the next stage of the publishing process, you can come back to your larger project and select another reader and run through these questions again.

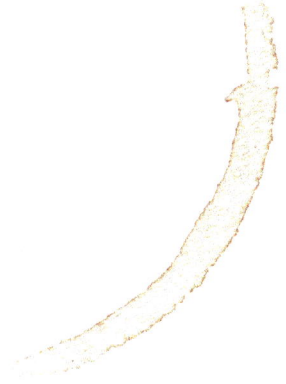

Refining a Specific Writing Product

Now that you have a clearer idea of the type of writing product you are aiming for and who you want to read it, you are at another kind of beginning: the beginning of a bounded project with a specific end. This (or the even later stage of a finished conference paper) is the beginning imagined in books like *Write Your Journal Article in 12 Weeks*.

Your writing process is no longer purely about your own intellectual satisfaction (although that is still important) but must now also take into account the particular standards of the conversation to which you would like to contribute and the particular characteristics of your potential reader. This project may result in multiple interim products on the way to your specific goal, each with slightly different standards.

Defining a specific goal may reawaken your fears and shake your confidence and trust. Do not allow your writing to be driven by fear. Trust that your potential reader will be interested in your writing, and that you can frame the writing product in such a way that you pique their interest. Trust that you can write something good enough to be published in the venue you are aiming for.

I use the term "good enough" deliberately. Many academics struggle with perfectionism. Your fear tells you that perfectionism is really just striving for excellence. It isn't. Perfectionism is a self-esteem issue. You are not publishing to prove how smart you are. You are publishing to communicate your ideas to a specific audience.

Perfectionism is also a form of all or nothing thinking; everything is either perfect or worthless. You cannot see gradations of better and worse: good enough becomes, as one critic put it, "the handmaiden of mediocrity". You can't identify priorities. Although you seek external validation, you will not trust it unless, paradoxically, it is scathing criticism. You may dismiss or argue with those who compliment your work. You may even rail against declining standards. Like Groucho Marx, you would not want to be a member of any club who would admit your work as good enough.

By using the term "good enough", I want to offer you a way out of that negative spiral. "Good enough" is not "the handmaiden of mediocrity" but rather a specification of what excellence looks like in a particular context. When you identify a particular potential reader and a specific context of publication, you can more clearly specify what the criteria for excellence are in that specific context. Those clear functional criteria will, in turn, allow you to determine when your writing is good enough. Although you will continue to develop your ideas and arguments as you write, your process shifts to one of refinement towards this concrete goal.

> Refinement is that process of adding only what's needed and removing everything that's not. It's about a certain precision. It's about making smart choices about what one's creation needs to do its job in the world. (Cairene MacDonald)

In a pattern similar to the earlier stages of this process, you may need to write more than you keep. To articulate the things that are particularly important to this audience, you may need to go through a process of writing things this audience isn't going to care much about and then deleting them. This doesn't mean that what you wrote is not important. It is just not that important to this audience. You may find it helpful to have a place to put all of the things you want to write that don't fit into this particular writing product. Remember, you will write other things for other audiences about this topic. Although you are currently focused on this particular writing product, you may find that you are generating material for another one at the same time. When you turn to that one, you will be pleasantly surprised to find out how much of it is already written.

For example, if you are writing a conference paper, you have limited time to talk about background and will focus your writing on your unique contribution.

In order to really work out what your contribution is, you may need to write quite a bit about the debate to which you are contributing. And then delete it all from the conference paper (or at least the oral version of it). When you come to write a journal article for a similar audience, you will bring much of that context back in to situate your argument.

Another example, unless you are well practiced in writing for non-academic audiences, you may need to write in a more academic style to develop and refine your arguments. You will then cut out or radically summarize a lot of things that academics care about but your non-academic audience is indifferent to (like the academic literature review), explain or replace terms that are well understood by your scholarly colleagues but not by others, and so on. Trying to write in plain language right away is likely to lead to an inability to write at all and / or feed your fear that you just can't do this.

Deciding on refinements

Curiosity is still your friend at this stage. Engage your curiosity about your reader. Verify your assumptions about what you need to write for this venue of publication or presentation.

Is this true?

Why are things done this way?

What is the underlying goal that this practice serves?

Is there another way to meet that goal?

Remind yourself of why this reader is interested in your work and how it will benefit them and their work.

What is the most important thing I want the reader to take away from reading this? Is that clearly communicated?

Have I situated my argument in the context the reader finds most important?

What does this reader expect to see in the writing?

Is the language I'm using familiar to this reader?

Is the language I'm using precise enough?

How can I adjust the language so that it retains the necessary precision but is more familiar?

Have I over-explained anything that is well known to this reader? If so, what is the necessary level of detail?

Is there anything I usually take for granted that this reader might need more explanation of?

Are all the claims I am making well supported by evidence? Have I checked? Is that clear to the reader?

What is Finished?

You may notice that as you approach "finished" you experience a kind of despair. It seems like what you are writing is banal, your contribution insignificant. The fear of not being good enough and not having anything original to say reaches a peak. You've spent all this time and achieved nothing of significance.

This is normal. It happens to everyone. The night is darkest before the dawn and all that. Once you've experienced this cycle a few times you can get better at spotting it and recognizing it for what it is. It never goes away, but it can become just a reminder of how close you are to finished.

Returning to the distinction between process and product can help make sense of this all too common experience. Writing is a cognitive process. Even while you had a specific goal in mind, the process did not cease to be important in and of itself. It was helping you grapple with complex ideas and evidence and articulate them clearly. You have created knowledge. And through the process of writing, you now know these things. Other people, who have not been through this process with you, can learn from the product you have created, which will in turn contribute to their own process of knowledge creation through writing.

Furthermore, your product may well feel "not quite finished" when you submit it (or even when it is published). As a cognitive process, writing raises more questions and new directions you could take the work. Those new questions and directions may appear as flaws or underdeveloped elements in the current writing-as-product. Often, the apparent flaws are invitations to submit this piece so you can get on with developing those underdeveloped elements in a new piece of writing. It is not easy to tell the difference between a need for further refinement and an invitation to begin a new piece. This particular writing product will be part of a larger body of work.

A literary example illustrates this distinction in more detail. In 2009, I attended a production of Ann-Marie MacDonald's *Belle Moral* at the National Arts Centre in Ottawa, Canada. The author's note in the program caught my attention.

> *Belle Moral: A Natural History* has its origins in an earlier play of mine called *The Arab's Mouth* ... After *The Arab's Mouth* premiered [in 1990], I knew that it was not quite finished and, in keeping with my experience as a playwright and collaborator, I fully expected to return to it. I got distracted, however, by another project which I thought would be a play but turned out to be a novel. *Fall On Your Knees* developed many of the themes and images that I had touched on in *The Arab's Mouth*, and I came to see the play as a progenitor — or, to change metaphors, as a kind of sketch book for the novel.

JO VAN EVERY

The novel and the later play may have their origins in the same original work, but they are very different, and equally excellent products. And yet, from the author's perspective the earlier play, and presumably the novel, felt "not quite finished". I am very glad that she produced/published them anyway. The world would not be a better place had she kept them in a folder until the "finished" piece was ready.

Different types of writing product have different standards for finished work. Writing which does not meet the standard required of a journal article may well be finished in the context of a blog post or a conference paper. Take this example: one of my academic friends published a blog post with the caveat that these were thoughts she hadn't quite straightened out yet. One of her other friends responded:

> I'm grateful this piece is not neat – it's just staring at me as a reminder for me to write, regardless of whether I feel like what I'm writing is a coherent whole or not. Because this piece obviously ISN'T a coherent whole, and yet it's still there asking me IMPORTANT questions about what it means ... [stuff about specific topic] And I have takes on many of these questions myself, and yet I'm super-nervous about sharing them because they're NOT fully-formed thoughts, and they only relate to my tiny little [specific] corner of the universe. (Chuck Pearson)

Remember you are publishing to contribute to a conversation. Writing-as-product may be part of a collaborative writing process that functions not as co-authorship but as a more asynchronous conversation in which all parties work out their ideas and arguments semi-publicly.

You don't have to have all the answers. And you don't have to have the definitive argument no one will disagree with. You need to have something to contribute to the conversation. It needs to be in a form that meets the standards of the publishing outlet you have chosen.

Are you finished?

Do you recognize this feeling that a project you've worked on for a long time is insignificant?

Do you have a project at that stage right now?

What shifts if you consider the possibility that this is a normal part of the process?

Here's a way to figure out if your project needs further refinement or if you just need to submit it and get on with writing something else.

List the elements that feel underdeveloped. For each of these elements ask,

Could you refine this element without radically changing the whole argument?

You may need to begin writing (in a new document) about just this element to figure out the answer. That is not a waste of time. It shouldn't take you long to figure out if this is a new piece or a refinement, at which point you can go back to your almost finished piece and proceed accordingly.

This question may also be helpful if your project gets stuck at an earlier point in the process. Sometimes the barrier to refining an argument is that you have two separate arguments intertwined in what you think is only one article. Separating them, and thinking of your writing in terms of multiple products, can get the writing flowing again.

Getting Another Perspective

As the beginning of the last section suggests, by the time you are close to finished it's hard to judge your own work. You are too familiar with it. Setting it aside to work on something else and coming back to it later helps. But it's also a good idea to get feedback from others. Luckily those two strategies combine really well.

Developing a network of colleagues who can give you feedback is crucial to a successful academic career. A key criterion for selecting people to ask for feedback is their ability to provide the type of feedback you need in a form you can use. You also want to screen out people who approach publishing from a position of fear. You want feedback that helps you submit sooner, not feedback that feeds your perfectionism and fear.

Learning to give and receive feedback, and knowing your own strengths and weaknesses, will make it easier to develop these networks. Reciprocity may be direct — you give feedback on a colleague's work in exchange for them giving feedback on yours — or diffuse — what goes around comes around.

Be clear and specific in your request. Do you want general feedback on whether the argument hangs together? Feedback on a particular section you are struggling with? A judgement about whether this is good enough to submit to a specific journal? Provide a reasonable timeline and make it easy for them to say no if they are too busy, if the kind of feedback you want isn't really their strength, or if they do not have sufficient knowledge or experience.

Knowing what kind of feedback you want will also help you decide who to ask. Your friend who can't see the inspirational message in that Facebook meme because of a misspelled word is an ideal person to have proof your article immediately prior to submission but is probably not the person to ask for feedback at the stage where you need confirmation that your main argument makes sense and you have the basic structure to support it. Some people prefer to provide big picture comments and aren't as good at helping you find exactly the right words, or proofreading. Sometimes you want a view on the overall coherence from a non-specialist. Sometimes you need feedback from someone with knowledge of the particular journal you plan to submit to.

Do not discount professional editors. The paid relationship is a very direct form of reciprocity. And a professional editor is not entangled in other aspects of your career. If you have professional development funds or grant funds, it is easier to consider hiring professional editing help. However, also consider the value of the time you save in both preparing manuscripts for submission and developing both your writing skill and your judgement about when something is good enough.

Early in your career, paying an editor from personal funds may be a worthwhile investment in your own professional development. Editors can help at all stages of the process from developing your ideas and structure right through to copy editing your final draft prior to submission. Some editors will combine editing with coaching.

Colleagues may be able to recommend an editor. There are also national and regional editors associations that provide directories of members. Look for an editor with experience editing for the type of publication you are aiming for, including experience of specific style guides. A professional editor could be particularly helpful as you move into publishing for non-academic audiences but there are also many professional editors who specialize in academic publishing.

Do you need another perspective?

Do you think this might be finished? Have you made a decision about where you want to submit it? If not, make that decision, review your draft again in the light of that decision. Then list your remaining doubts or questions and give it to a colleague for feedback.

If you know you aren't close to finished but you are stuck, you've tried the questions in the relevant section of this *Short Guide*, and you're still not sure what to do, then you need another perspective.

What would be most helpful at this stage? Can you specify what kind of feedback you'd like? Do you need someone to read it? Or do you need to talk it over with someone? Once you are clear on what you need, identify a good person to ask and ask them.

Submission, Revision, Publication

The scholarly writing process does not end with submission to a journal or book publisher. Just as there are many beginnings to your writing, there are also many endings.

The peer review process in academic publishing is a more formal process of providing feedback and guiding final refinements. The standard for submission is high, and the feedback you sought prior to submission will help you meet that high standard. However, you should expect to make further refinements prior to publication. Your goal when submitting is to receive a "revise and resubmit" decision.

Once you receive that decision, you will have clear guidance from the editor about what good enough looks like. You will use the reviewers comments and the journal editor's specific guidance to make your final revisions. This is still your article. It may be that some of the feedback you receive will not go into the revised version. It is not uncommon for reviewers suggestions to conflict, in which case you select the approach you will take and explain your choices to the editor. Perhaps a specific suggestion would be better dealt with as a separate publication. If this is the case, you need to communicate your decision to the editor when you resubmit. You can then decide whether writing that other paper is a priority or not. (If you do, you can acknowledge the anonymous reviewer in a footnote for suggesting this line of argument.)

Even a rejection from a specific publication, while painful, can be treated as further feedback on your paper. You should not resubmit a rejected paper to the same publication, but the reviewers comments can help you make decisions about a more appropriate venue, and even whether further refinements are required when you change venue. The network of colleagues you used to provide pre-submission feedback may help you make judgements about what you do and don't need to do at this stage. You may find it helpful to select a back-up journal earlier in the process. Then if you are rejected, you already have a plan for how to move forward.

Many non-academic publishing processes also have editorial input between submission and publication. They may even have a process of pitching to get agreement in principle prior to submission. Getting expert guidance on how different publishing processes work, from those who have successfully published there or from editors who have experience working with those publications, is invaluable.

And You Keep Writing

I have argued that scholarly writing is more than merely the production of specific publications. The term "writing" refers to both the process of translating the ideas in your head into words on a page and to the products of that process. Writing is a cognitive process in which you develop and articulate your ideas. Any particular publication is part of a larger body of scholarly work.

Curiosity, arguably the foundation of all academic work, can also be directed at the process itself, allowing you to work with the powerful emotions that surface as you write, to take your writing in different directions, and to focus your writing on specific products for specific audiences.

It is not helpful to think of writing as something you do only when you have a particular product in mind. Not everything you write will be something you want to share with others. It is not a waste of time to write things that will never become conference papers, or articles. It is not a waste of time to write unsuccessful grant proposals; or book proposals that you decide not to submit to a publisher. If what you write helps move your thinking forward, it is worthwhile. Moving your thinking forward often looks like going off on a tangent, or even failing.

It is much more helpful to think of writing as a practice, analogous to a yoga practice or a spiritual practice. Your writing practice will adapt to your particular context and evolve over time. I have written another *Short Guide, Finding Time for your Scholarly Writing*, which provides more detail about what a writing practice might look like and how you might use different kinds of writing time to build a practice that works for you, and reflect on and adjust that practice periodically.

Notes & References

Introduction: The Academic Writing Studio (AcademicWritingStudio.co.uk) is a membership site I run offering online resources & community as well as a synchronous Meeting With Your Writing weekly.

Beginnings: I use the term "gremlins" to refer to the voices in your head, also know as internal critics, monsters, and similar. I acknowledge the influence of Havi Brooks of The Fluent Self (fluentself.com) in my usage and in my suggestions for dealing with them. If you find it helpful there is a (free) printable Gremlin Colouring Page on my website: jovanevery.ca/gremlin-colouring-page

The phrase "shitty first draft" comes from Anne Lamott's *Bird by Bird* (Anchor Books, 1980).

Rohan Maitzen's review of Elizabeth Gilbert's *Big Magic*, "Pen and Tell Her" was published in *Open Letters Monthly* November 1, 2015 openlettersmonthly.com/pen-and-tell-her

Moving Your Project Forward: More information on Scrivener is available at literatureandlatte.com; on Evernote at evernote.com. There are other applications which will do similar things. My choice to mention these two products is arbitrary.

From Process to Product: The Margaret Atwood quotation is from a talk she gave February 15, 2011 entitled The Publishing Pie. A recording is available on YouTube youtu.be/-6iMBf6Ddjk

The passage from Dorothy Smith is published in *The Everyday World as Problematic: a feminist sociology*, 1988, Open University Press, pp 45-46.

Refining a Specific Writing Product: *Write Your Journal Article in 12 Weeks* is by Wendy Belcher and published by Sage (2009). It is used here as an example of a type of writing advice book. There are other similar books. My choice to use this example is arbitrary.

The phrase "handmaiden of mediocrity" is used by Rohan Maitzen in "Pen and Tell Her" (*Open Letters Monthly* November 1, 2015 www.openlettersmonthly.com/pen-and-tell-her).

The quotation from Cairene MacDonald is part of a blog post "Refinement vs Perfectionism" published at Third Hand Works, July 20, 2010 thirdhandworks.com/2010/07/refinement-vs-perfectionism

What is Finished?: The quotation from Ann-Marie MacDonald is taken from the "Afterword" of the published edition of the play *Belle Moral: A Natural History*, 2008, Vintage Canada, pp. 153-54

The Chuck Pearson quotation is from personal communication on Facebook and is used with permission.

Acknowledgements

This Short Guide began as what I thought would be a series of blog posts engaging with Rohan Maitzen's review of Elizabeth Gilbert's *Big Magic* in *Open Letters Monthly*. Gilbert's definition of a creative life as one "that is driven more strongly by curiosity than by fear" strikes me as as good a definition of academic work as any. That initial idea developed into something that looks quite different from what I initially envisioned, which seems appropriate. I am grateful to Jane Jones, of Up In Consulting, for her editorial input as I clarified this. She helped me apply the ideas I write about in this Short Guide to my own process.

The ideas presented here have developed through the work I do with my clients, both individually and as members of the Academic Writing Studio and participants in A Meeting With Your Writing. I would also like to thank Sarah Lacy, Amy Crook, and Wendy Cholbi for providing regular opportunities to talk about my ideas and for encouragement to write them.

Helen Kara's decision to publish a series of e-books about the PhD process (available at knowmorepublishing.com) prompted me to think about sharing my work in this way. Her recommendation of the Alliance of Independent Authors (allianceindependentauthors.org) was particularly helpful, and I thank ALLi for the advice and support they provide.

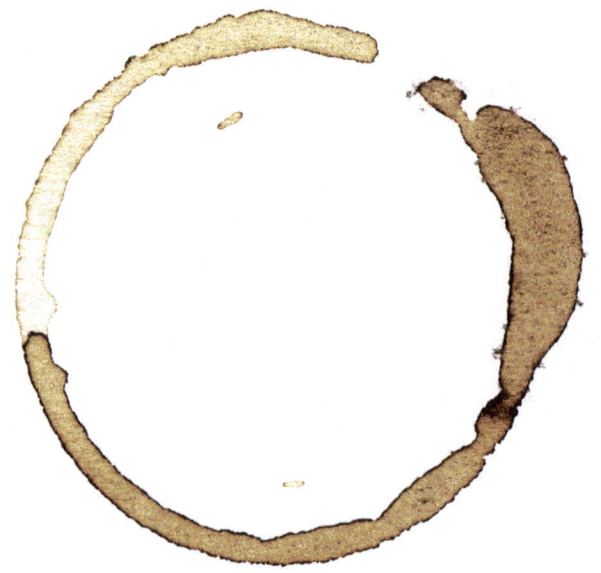

About the Author

Jo VanEvery transforms academic lives from surviving to thriving. She used to be an academic sociologist and then a program officer for a funding agency. Now she helps you juggle your myriad responsibilities, provides a structure so you can get more writing done, helps you clarify your vision and make a plan for the next part of the path towards it, and boosts your confidence so you can do the work that makes your heart sing. You can read more of her writing on her website, jovanevery.ca; follow her on Twitter, twitter.com/JoVanEvery ; or like her Facebook page, facebook.com/JoVEAcademicCareerCoach/ .

Also by Jo VanEvery:

The Principles of Juggling: A Picture Book for Academics (ISBN 978-1-912040-71-1)

Finding Time for your Scholarly Writing (Short Guides, vol 2) (ISBN 978-1-912040-70-4 pb 978-1-912040-69-8 ebook)

Coming Soon:

Scholarly Publishing (A Short Guide)

Peer Review (A Short Guide)

Saying No Yes (A Short Guide)

Optimizing Focus (A Short Guide)

Lightning Source UK Ltd.
Milton Keynes UK
UKHW021028080720
366178UK00006B/132

The Scholarly Writing Process

A Short Guide

Jo VanEvery, PhD

The Scholarly Writing Process
Short Guides vol 1

1st edition © 2016 Jo VanEvery

2nd edition © 2018 Jo VanEvery

ISBN 978-1-912040-64-3

Cover & Interior Design: Amy Crook

JO VAN EVERY

Preface:
How to Use This Short Guide

The *Short Guides* series is intended to help you when you are stuck. Each *Short Guide* focuses on one area of your academic life, complementing advice with writing prompts to help you apply that advice in your own particular circumstances.

The Scholarly Writing Process (A Short Guide) focuses on writing as a process, from your initial curiosity about a topic or question, through the development of arguments, the identification of potential readers, the specification of a product, and the refinement of your writing for publication in a specific form.

I suggest reading through the guide once to get a sense of how the whole thing fits together. Then leave it somewhere accessible. Whenever you are stuck with a writing project, go to the part that speaks to what you need in that moment. Use the questions in that section to get things moving.

I encourage you to actually write out answers to the questions. You are a writer. Writing is how you process your thoughts. Depending on where you are stuck, it might even be appropriate to write your answers in your project document.

Getting stuck is a normal part of the writing process, even for experienced writers. My aim in publishing this *Short Guide* is to help you generate new writing projects, keep your writing projects moving forward, and ensure that your writing process results in publications. Keep this guide close by and refer to it whenever you need to.

Enjoy your writing!

JO VAN EVERY

Table of Contents:

Preface: How to Use This Short Guide iii

Writing as Process & Product 1

Beginnings.. 6

Moving Your Project Forward 11

From Process to Product:
Who Are You Writing For?........................... 17

Determining Which Writing Products
to Prioritize.. 23

Refining a Specific Writing Product 28

What is Finished? 33

Getting Another Perspective 38

Submission, Revision, Publication............. 42

And You Keep Writing 44

Notes & References 46

Acknowledgements 49

About the Author 51

Jo Van Every